apple

astronaut

awake

asleep

arrow

ant

acorn

ambulance

butterfly

bus

ball

boy

bee

bicycle

bird

bubbles

bath

bear

crayons

car

cow

clown

carrot

crown

cake

caterpillar

cat

dolphin

dragonfly

duckling

dinosaur

duck

dog

doll

dry

elephant

eagle

egg

envelope

ear

eye

engine

friends

fish

fingers

frog

feather

flower

fruit

family

gloves

grapes

goldfish

giraffe

goat

goose

grass

gate

hamster

helicopter

hat

hairbrush

hearts

hippo

hot-air
balloons

horse

icicles

insects

ice cream

ice skating

iguana

ice

jellyfish

jigsaw puzzle

juice

jump

jacket

jeans

jam

L

lime

lemon

lamb

lamp

letters

lettuce

lion

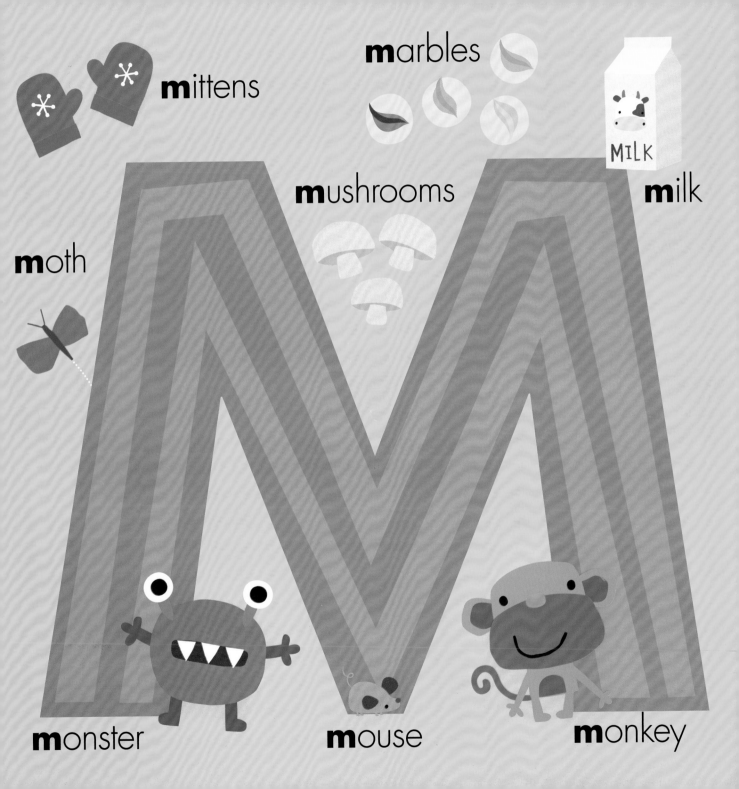

mittens

marbles

milk

MILK

moth

mushrooms

monster

mouse

monkey

necklace

night

nest

nuts

newt

nectarine

nurse

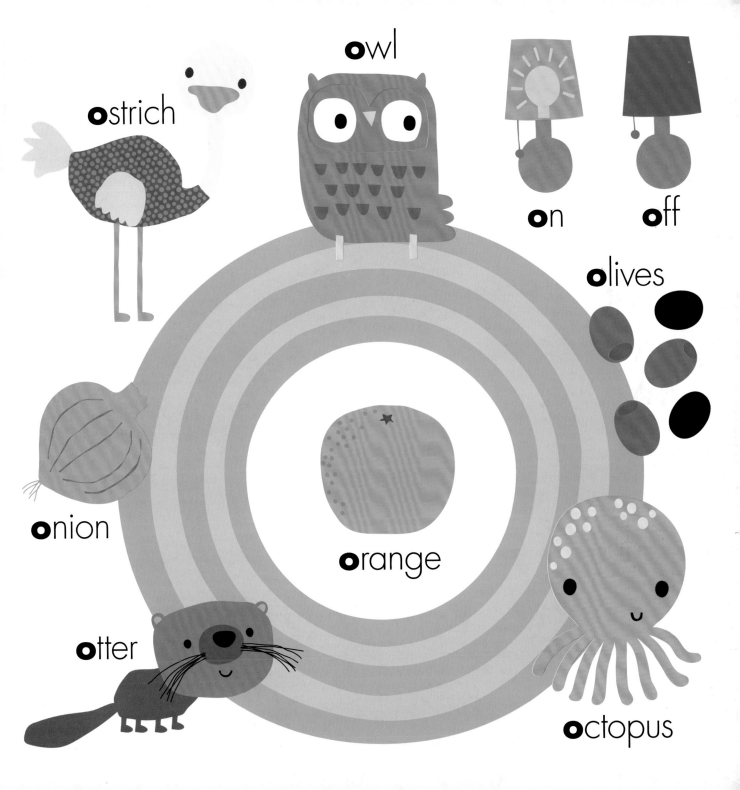

ostrich

owl

on

off

olives

onion

orange

octopus

otter

penguin

pizza

paper

pear

police car

POLICE

pig

pond

piglets

rug

rocket

race car

robot

rhino

rabbit

shoe

sheep

sssss
snake

shark

sandwich

snail

spider

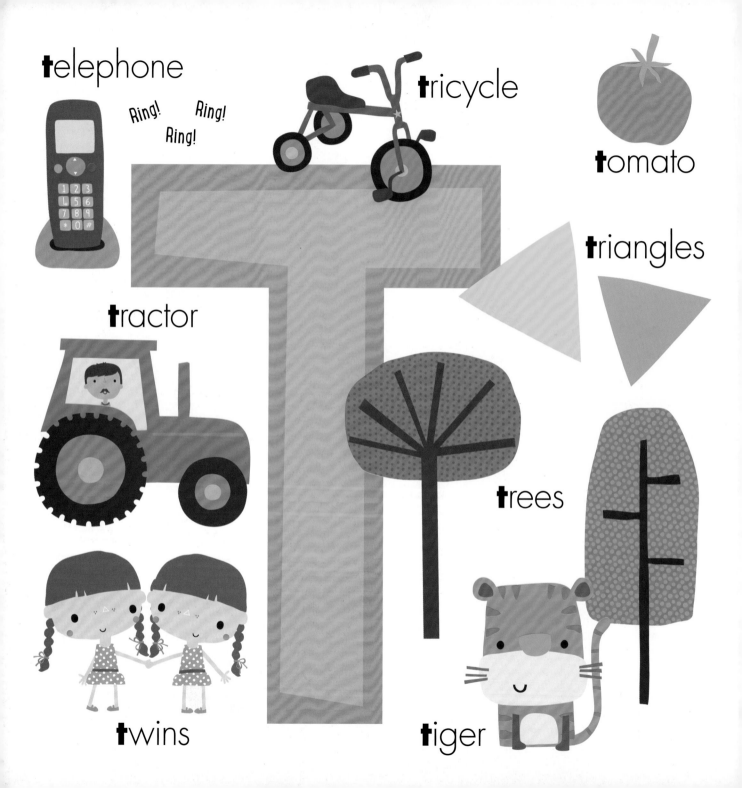

telephone

Ring! *Ring!*
Ring!

tricycle

tomato

triangles

tractor

trees

twins

tiger

unicorn

unicycle

umbrella

underwater

up

underground

vulture

vase

A E I
O U
vowels

vine

van

vegetables

wand

woodpecker

water

web

watermelon

whale

wet

x-ray

yak

yellow

xylophone

zebras

yo-yo